Ultimate FACTIVITY Collection
ANIMALS

Create your own book about the amazing world of animals

LONDON, NEW YORK, MUNICH,
MELBOURNE, AND DELHI

Project Editor Laura Palosuo
US Editor Margaret Parrish
Senior Designer Clare Shedden
Designers Charlotte Bull, Gemma Fletcher,
Ria Holland, Hannah Moore
Design Assistance Jane Ewart, Glenda Fisher, Elaine Hewson,
Clare Marshall, Claire Patané, Yumiko Tahata
Editorial Assistance Ellie de Rose, Carrie Love
Consultant Dr Kim Dennis-Bryan
Jacket Designers Ria Holland, Rosie Levine, Natasha Rees
Illustrators Charlotte Bull, Helen Dodsworth, Chris Howker,
Barney Ibbotson, Jake McDonald, Hannah Moore, Yumiko Tahata

Pre-Production Producer Sarah Isle
Senior Producer Alex Bell
Creative Technical Support Sonia Charbonnier
Managing Editor Penny Smith
Senior Managing Art Editor Marianne Markham
Publisher Mary Ling
Creative Director Jane Bull

First American Edition, 2014
Published in the United States by DK Publishing
4th floor, 345 Hudson Street, New York, New York 10014

14 15 16 17 18   10 9 8 7 6 5 4 3 2 1
001–196310–07/14

A catalog record for this book is available from the Library of Congress.
ISBN: 978-1-4654-1655-1

DK books are available at special discounts when purchased in bulk for sales promotions,
premiums, fund-raising, or educational use. For details, contact: DK Publishing Special
Markets, 345 Hudson Street, New York, New York 10014 or SpecialSales@dk.com.

Printed and bound in China by L. Rex Printing Co., Ltd.
Discover more at **www.dk.com**

Creepy, crawly, slimy, scaly

The creatures in this section may seem creepy, but only a few are actually dangerous to humans. Many of them help humans, for example, by eating waste material.

FIND
these pictures on pages 4–17 and write the page numbers in the boxes.

page _____

page _____

page _____

page _____

page _____

page _____

Don't forget to put your stickers in first.

2

Did you know?

FIND

stickers to match the animal shapes on this page and stick them down.

Spider

When a spider's web needs to be repaired, the spider will eat the web and start all over again.

Scorpion

A scorpion attacks its prey using its claws and tail. The venom from some species can paralyze a person's heart.

Honeybee

Honeybees may flap their wings up to 11,000 times a minute. This is what creates a buzzing sound.

Millipede

The word millipede means "one thousand legs" but the most that has ever been counted is 750.

Cockroach

Cockroaches are incredibly tough. They can survive without eating anything for a whole month, although they can only live one week without water.

Dragonfly eyes have 30,000 lenses

Dragonfly

Dragonflies are the world's fastest flying insects. Their speed helps them catch their prey.

Quizzes

How many bugs?

For every one person alive, there are 200 million insects. At least nine out of 10 of all the animal species on Earth are bugs. There are too many to count... until now!

COUNT

the **grasshoppers** and **crickets**.

Jump to it!

Write in the numbers

Find the stickers

Grasshopper

Desert locust

Katydid

Facts about...

Crickets and grasshoppers

These jumpy insects have extra-long hindlegs to leap around tall grass. Crickets rub their wings together to "sing" and attract a mate. Chirp!

Beetles

Beetles are insects with hard front wings that aren't used for flying. Instead, the wings protect them like armor. One-third of all insects in the world are beetles.

Stag beetle   June bug   Ladybug

COUNT

the **beetles** beetling around on these two pages.

COUNT

up all the creeping **caterpillars** you can find.

Caterpillars

Caterpillars may look like walking worms, but they are actually butterflies and moths in the making. They eat leaves, shed their skin as they grow, and eventually become butterflies.

Swallowtail caterpillar

Fritillary caterpillar

Hawk moth caterpillar

Some species of chameleon change color to blend into their surroundings. This helps to camouflage them, but there's more to chameleons than meets the eye.

Now you see me, now you don't

Changing color

Chameleons don't just change color for camouflage. They also use it to communicate with other chameleons—to show their mood, for example.

Chameleons can look in two different directions at the same time!

What a catch
Chameleons' tongues can be **as long as their bodies**. This comes in handy when they need to catch insects for dinner!

COLOR

the chameleon, then use similar colors to blend him into the background.

Spinning spiders

Many spiders build strong and detailed webs to catch insects that they can eat. When something gets caught in the web, the spider feels the vibrations and then attacks!

FINISH the spider's web below. Then stick the missing spiders to the right.

Use stickers to add the spider's catch to the web.

Tangle webs can cover the top of a shrub and are very difficult to escape from.

Black widow spider

Tangle web

Are webs all the same?

There are many types of web and different spiders build different types of web.

Orb webs are the most common. They are flat and round and made in a spiral shape.

Orb weaver

Orb web

House spider

Funnel webs are usually found in hidden corners. Spiders hide in them and wait for prey.

Funnel web

Sheet webs get their name because they are woven flat, like bed sheets.

Sheet web spider

Sheet web

I'm a house spider. I build webs in corners and windowsills.

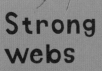

Tarantulas

Tarantulas don't spin webs to catch their prey. Instead, they wait and attack. Tarantulas mainly eat insects, but they also catch frogs, mice, and small birds.

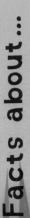

Facts about...

Strong webs

Scientists estimate that spider silk is five times stronger than steel of the same weight and thickness.

Sneaky Snakes

Snakes are sneaky hunters. They slither silently toward their prey and then snatch it suddenly. Some kill with their venomous bite. Others squeeze prey to death.

MATCH the snake stickers to the shapes and read all about the snakes.

CORN SNAKE
Length: 4–6 feet (1–1.8 meters)
Habitat: Overgrown fields, under logs and rocks, on trees, or in buildings
Venomous: Not venomous

GREEN TREE PYTHON
Length: 6–8 feet (1.8–2.4 meters)
Habitat: Rain forest
Venomous: Not venomous
Superb at hiding in leaves

GRASS SNAKE
Length: 4–7 feet (1.2–2 meters)
Habitat: Grassy ground near water
Venomous: Not venomous
Eats frogs, toads, and worms

GREEN ANACONDA
Length: Up to 19½–33 feet
(6–10 meters)
Habitat: Swamps and
rain forests
Venomous: Not venomous

KING COBRA
Length: Up to 10–16½ feet
(3–5 meters)
Habitat: Asian forests, often
near water
Venomous: Deadly to humans,
but rarely come in contact

MILK SNAKE
Length: 2–5 feet
(0.4–2 meters)
Habitat: Forests, prairies,
grasslands, near rivers and
streams, and rocky hillsides
Venomous: Not venomous

COMMON BOA
Length: Up to 13 ft
(4 meters)
Habitat: Rain forest
Venomous: Not venomous
Coils around victims and
squeezes them to death

A snake's wide jaws
are for swallowing
prey whole.

Common boa

A snake's scaly skin
is smooth and
slippery, but dry.

**DIAMONDBACK
RATTLESNAKE**
Length: Up to 7 ft (2 meters)
Habitat: Rocky ground
Venomous: Yes. It can be
deadly to humans

SIDE WINDER
Length: 2–3 feet
(45–80 centimeters)
Habitat: Desert
Venomous: Yes. It can be
deadly to humans

11

The amazing gecko

If you ever visit somewhere warm, watch out for these amazing, pop-eyed, multicolored lizards—their sticky toes allow them to walk up walls and across ceilings.

A gecko's sticky feet work best when they are dry.

Crazy colors

Geckos come in an amazing range of patterns. Some can even change color!

We can climb up smooth and slippery windows!

Climbing walls

The reason geckos can climb walls is that the pads on their feet are covered in millions of tiny branching hairs that can cling to any surface.

Facts about...

COMPLETE the gecko jigsaw and decorate the page with stickers. Then try the quiz.

1 A gecko can shed its tail to escape from danger. Then it grows a new one!

TRUE FALSE

Leopard geckos are camouflaged to hide in deserts.

2 Flying geckos use flaps of webbed skin to glide when they jump from trees.

TRUE FALSE

Challenges

Electric blue geckos live in tropical Africa.

3 Geckos can't blink so they lick their eyes to clean them.

TRUE FALSE

4 The marine gecko is as big as a dolphin and lives underwater.

TRUE FALSE

13

Colorful frogs

Poison dart frogs are tropical tree frogs. Central and South American tribes people from the rain forests of Costa Rica and Brazil use the frogs' toxic skin to poison their hunting arrows.

Beware! Toxic!

Bright colors on a frog's skin warn predators that they are poisonous. Some harmless frogs look so similar that predators mistake them for poison frogs and leave them alone.

GO WILD

when you color in the frogs! The brighter, the better.

Give this one red and blue legs.

COUNT up all the frogs you can see on these pages.

The bright colors warn other animals they are poisonous.

Facts about...

Frogs

Poison dart frogs are only 1–2½in (2–6cm) long. They eat small insects that they catch with their long tongues.

This is the actual size of this poison dart frog!

Watch out! Don't come near me!

15

Creepy-crawlies are everywhere

Creepy-crawlies live in a variety of places, from dark underground burrows to freshwater. They creep, climb, wriggle, and slither their way around.

FILL

the scene with creepy-crawly stickers and add mites to the magnifying glass.

These Red Velvet mites are hard to see.

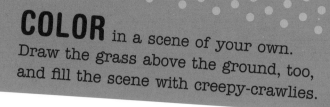

COLOR in a scene of your own.
Draw the grass above the ground, too,
and fill the scene with creepy-crawlies.

Challenges

Cute and cuddly

Nothing is cuter and more cuddly than a furry animal. Although many of these animals live in the wild, some live in zoos. Others live with humans as work animals or pets

Don't forget to put your stickers in first.

page _____

page _____

FIND

these pictures on pages 20–33 and write the page numbers in the boxes.

page _____

page _____

page _____

page _____

Color in the background to match the giraffe's coat.

Spotted fawns blend in with the leafy forest floor.

Help me hide

Because all zebras have the **same pattern** it is harder for predators to pick out one when the whole group runs away.

This pygmy marmoset hugs a tree trunk and is difficult to spot.

COLOR
the backgrounds to help these animals blend into their surroundings.

Cat quiz

Time for a nap yet?

tabby cat

With an agile body, acute senses, lightning-quick reflexes, and camouflage colors, a cat is an ideal hunter. It also likes to snuggle!

1
A cat's sense of smell is twice as keen as a human's.

TRUE   FALSE

short-haired cat

ANSWER
the true or false questions on these pages.

Cat coats

Cats keep clean by licking their coats. Although cats are **furry**, hot weather isn't a problem for them because they hunt at night and rest during the day.

Facts about...

Purring
Purring usually shows that a cat is happy, but a deep purr can mean the cat is startled or upset.

long-haired cat

2
Whiskers help a cat feel its way.

TRUE   FALSE

FALSE?

3

Cats begin to purr at just two days old.

TRUE ○○ FALSE

Kittens

Kittens love to play! They chase toys and **play-fight** to practice **skills** they would have needed in the wild—to hunt for food and fight for their territory.

4

Cats nap for an average of 13 to 14 hours per day.

TRUE ○○ FALSE

5

Cats have an extra eyelid to keep each eye clean and moist.

TRUE ○○ FALSE

Where's my mommy?

21

Rabbits live in underground warrens. A warren can be as big as a tennis court, with tunnels leading to chambers for adults, fur-lined nests for babies, and secret emergency exits.

Rabbit warren
maze

START

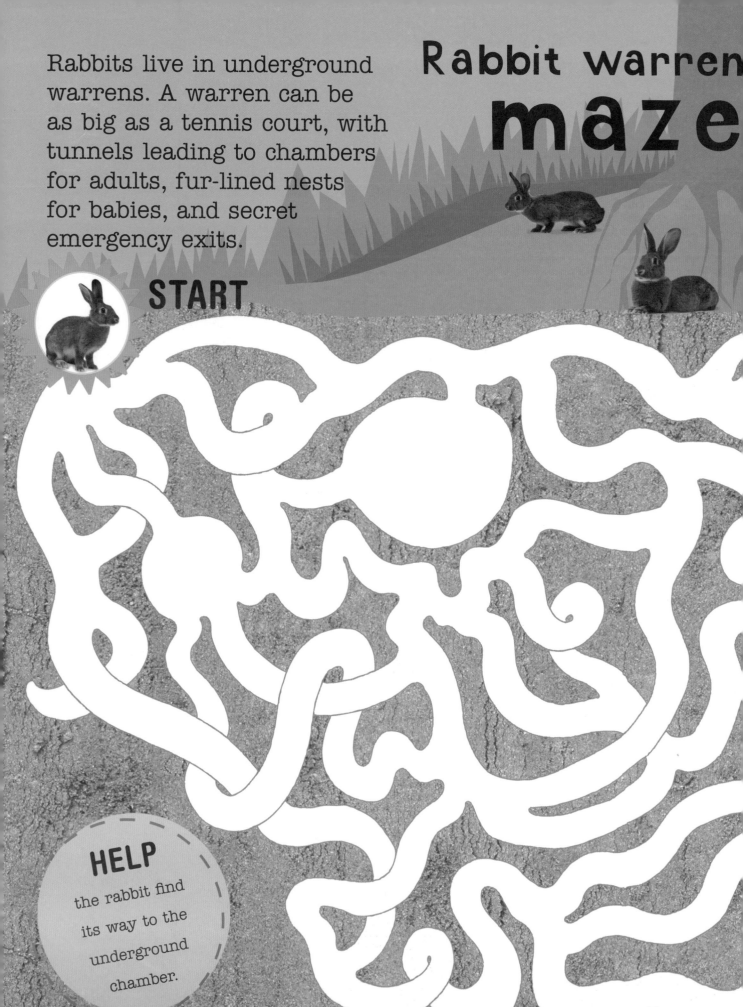

HELP
the rabbit find its way to the underground chamber.

Add more rabbits to the scene above and below ground.

END

Facts about...

Droppings

Rabbits eat grass and plants, which can be difficult to digest. To get all the nutrients from them, rabbits eat some of their own droppings so that the food passes through their intestines twice.

Dwarf rabbit

The dwarf rabbit is a special breed of rabbit that people keep as pets. They are about half the weight of common wild rabbits.

Find the missing rabbit stickers.

Angora rabbit

The fur of the angora rabbit is so long and soft that it's used to make an expensive kind of yarn, called angora.

Lop-eared rabbit

Most rabbits have upright ears to listen for danger, but lop-eared rabbits have long, droopy ears that make them popular as pets.

23

Dalmatian
fun

Famous for their unique **spotted** coats and playful personalities, dalmatians are much-loved family pets. How much do you know about them?

The great Dalmatian quiz

3
Dalmatians even have spots inside their **mouths**.

TRUE FALSE

2
Dalmatians were once thought to come from a historical region called **Dalmatia**.

TRUE FALSE

4
Dalmatians are relatives of spotted **leopards**.

TRUE FALSE

1
Dalmatians are born with black coats that **turn white and spotted** over time.

TRUE FALSE

5
Dalmatians all have exactly the **same number** of spots.

TRUE FALSE

Almost identical twins

There are six differences between these two pictures. Can you **spot** them all?

Woof, woof!

Newborn puppies can sleep up to **16 hours a day**

Dalmatians guarded horse-drawn fire trucks through the streets of London, England. They protected the trucks from thieves!

Cuddly koalas

Eucalyptus leaves

Koalas look like teddy bears, but they aren't bears at all. They're marsupials—animals that carry babies in a pouch. They live in Australia and are good at climbing trees.

Piggyback ride
Baby koalas are smaller than grapes when they're born. They spend six to seven months inside the pouch with their eyes closed. Then they spend six months riding on Mom's back.

A young koala is called a joey

STICK
the koalas in the eucalyptus trees and color in the leaves.

Baby animals quiz

Many animals protect and care for their babies and form a deep bond with them. Parents like to keep their babies close.

USE your stickers to reunite the baby animals with their parents.

Lions live in family groups called prides. This lion and lioness have lost their cub.

A baby horse or pony is called a foal until it is one year old. Horses can walk shortly after being born.

This dog is a Labrador

Young goats are called kids. They are born with horn buds that start to grow after 2–3 weeks.

Dogs have puppies in litters of about five or six. The world record for litter size is held by a Neapolitan mastiff. She had 24 puppies.

Female sheep are called ewes and their babies are lambs. A group of sheep is called a flock, herd, or mob.

Even a newborn giraffe is taller than most men. This giraffe should have no trouble finding its baby.

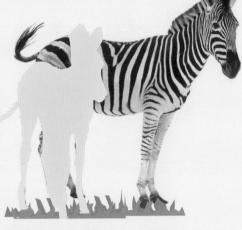

A baby wallaby is about as big as your fingertip when it's born. It crawls into a pouch of skin on it's mother's stomach where it develops.

Zebras can live for 10–20 years in the wild. In zoos, they have been known to live for up to 40 years.

Many young deer are born with white spots to help them hide from predators.

Cats like to rest. On average, cats spend two-thirds of each day asleep.

A female pig (called a sow) can have as many as 12 piglets in her litter, though the record is 35!

An elephant is pregnant for almost two years before its baby is born.

Male and female swans usually mate for life. Their babies are called cygnets.

Elephant babies hold on to their mom's tail with their trunks so they don't get lost.

Husky race

In sled-dog racing, teams of dogs pull sleds through snow and ice. The lead dogs are at the front. One or two swing dogs help the team around curves. The rest are team dogs. Mush! Mush!

FIND

which team wins and which teams end up in the doghouse.

Green team

Blue team

Red team

Facts about... Husky dogs

Huskies have very thick coats and they are strong and agile, making them good sled dogs. Huskies pulled the sleds of polar explorers!

TRUE OR FALSE?
IN RACES, SLED DOGS WEAR SHOES TO PROTECT THEIR FEET AGAINST SHARP ICE.

Facts about...

The lingo
There are special words that are used in dog sledding.

Mush! Go!
Gee! Turn right!
Haw! Turn left!
Whoa! Stop!
Mushing
Dog sledding

WHICH TEAM REACHES THE NORTH POLE AND WINS THE CUP?

NORTH POLE

DOG HOUSE

Pet store

STICK the pets into their correct homes to fill up this pet store scene.

Goldfish were one of the first types of fish to be kept as pets.

Parakeets are popular because they mimic speech.

Hamsters tend to sleep during the day and are awake at night.

Despite their name, guinea pigs are not part of the pig family.

Rabbits live in a special cage called a "hutch."

Puppies spend the majority of their time sleeping, eating, and playing.

DRAW the inside of a pet store. Which pets would you sell and how would you display them?

Gliders and **fliers**

Discover the world of creatures that can take to the air. It's not just birds that can rise above the ground—some fish and cuddly creatures can, too.

Don't forget to put your stickers in first.

page _____

page _____

FIND

these pictures on pages 36–49 and write the page numbers in the boxes.

page _____

page _____

page _____

page _____

Getting about

PLACE the stickers on the correct animals and answer the questions below.

Can I fly?

YES ◯ NO ◯

1 Penguin
Penguins are fast, graceful swimmers, but on land they waddle.

Can I glide?

YES ◯ NO ◯

2 Draco lizard
Draco lizards are also known as "flying lizards" because they can glide in the air.

Can I fly?

YES ◯ NO ◯

3 Kiwi
Kiwi birds are flightless birds that live in New Zealand. They have wings, but no flight muscles to allow them to fly.

Can I fly?

YES ◯ NO ◯

4 Ostrich
Ostriches can't fly because they are too heavy. They can, however, run at speeds up to 40 mph (70 kph).

Can I fly?

YES ◯ NO ◯

5 Jewel beetle
Jewel beetles will fly toward a forest fire, rather than away from it because they lay their eggs in burned wood.

Can I glide?

YES ◯ NO ◯

6 Flying fish
Flying fish have large, winglike fins that allow them to glide above the water's surface.

The big penguin count

Penguins aren't able to fly, but they make up for it by being excellent swimmers. That's definitely easier than walking around on slippery ice all day!

TRUE OR FALSE?
PENGUINS CAN BE FOUND CHILLING OUT AT BOTH THE NORTH AND SOUTH POLE.

COUNT the number of Rockhopper penguins you can find.

Write in the number of Rockhopper penguins on the page

Find penguin stickers to stick here

Facts about...

Rockhopper penguins

Known for their crest of **yellow and black feathers**, at only 20in (50cm) tall, Rockhoppers are one of the smallest species of penguin.

Humboldt penguins

Named after the explorer Alexander von Humboldt, these penguins have black and white heads with **a pink patch** by their bills.

King penguins

Recognizable by their bright **orange ear patches**, King penguins are the second largest of all penguin species.

COUNT

the number of Humboldt penguins you can find.

There are 17 different species of penguin worldwide.

COUNT

the number of King penguins you can find.

Games

37

In fine feather

A bird's brightly colored feathers help it to attract a mate or to blend into its habitat. The male's colors are usually brighter than the female's.

COLOR in the birds using the number key and finish drawing the peacock's tail.

1
2
3
4
5
6
7

Kingfisher

Sun parakeet

Gouldian finch

Blue and gold macaw

Cuvier's toucan

Roseate spoonbill

Australian king parrot

Flamingo

Flamingos get their pink color from the food they eat.

Scarlet macaw

A peackock's very long tail is called a "train."

Peacocks

A baby peacock is called a **peachick**, and a female peacock is a **peahen**. A peahen picks its mate (the peacock) by the width of its tail and the number of "eyespots" on it!

Finish this peacock's plumage

Color the finished peacock, too!

A-maze-ing bats

Bats are the only mammals that can fly. They are nocturnal, meaning they are awake at night. During the day, they sleep upside down in colonies with other bats.

START

GUIDE

the bat home. It uses echolocation to find its way.

Flying horseshoe bat

Echolocation

Bats can't see in the dark, but their hearing is superb. Some bats hunt by making sounds that bounce off prey and objects as an **echo**, telling the bat which way to go. This is called **echolocation**.

The bat sends out sound waves.

Sound waves bounce off the prey and back toward the bat.

Batty banquet

Many bats eat insects, some eat fruit, and some, namely the vampire bat, drink the blood of sleeping animals. Tasty!

END

Zzz...

Add more sleeping bats to the cave roof using your stickers.

Bird-watching

Some people like to observe and listen to birds. This is a hobby known as bird-watching. Bird-watchers often need to identify birds from a distance.

USE the information below to identify the birds flying in the sky.

1. We like to fly in formation. We are...
....

2. I carry fish in my big beak. I'm a...
....

Eagle
These powerful birds build their nests in tall trees or on high cliffs. Eagles have excellent eyesight and sharp beaks and claws that they use to catch their prey.

Flamingo
With their pink feathers and curved necks, flamingos are easy to spot. They can stand in water on one of their long, thin legs—this stops them from getting cold quickly.

Puffin
These small, black-and-white birds spend most of their lives at sea. They eat small fish and rest on waves when they're not swimming or diving for food.

4. We like to fly up high. We are…

....

3. I have a very long neck and legs. I'm a…

....

5. I have a sharp, hooked beak. I'm an…

....

6. I have a brightly colored beak. I'm a…

....

Geese

Long-necked geese are famous for migrating in formation in the winter months. They communicate by honking at each other. They live near water.

Pelican

These long-beaked birds are well known for their throat pouches, which they use to scoop up fish. Pelicans live by water and stay in groups known as colonies.

Swifts

These medium-sized birds are among the fastest fliers on Earth. They have small beaks and short tails, and they like to fly in groups high in the sky.

Un-bee-lievable!

A honeybee hive is a-buzz with activity. Worker bees fly in and out collecting pollen and nectar from flowers to turn into honey. Others look after the hive.

FOLLOW the clues and stick flowers on the three correct squares in the grid.

	1	2	3	4
A				
B				
C				
D				
E				

Waggle dance

A bee finds flowers far from the hive.

It flies home and does a dance to show others where they are.

This way!

Honeybees work together to collect nectar and pollen from flowers. If a bee finds a good spot, it will fly back and do a **waggle dance** to show the others which way to fly and for how long.

Use the clues to find the flowers

2 From the hive, fly left to the signpost. Then fly up two squares.

1 From the hive, fly up one square. Then fly to the left until you cross the road.

3 From the hive, fly straight up over all the farmer's fields. Then fly one square to the left.

Stick the queen bee onto her throne. Add worker bees to the honeycomb.

The bees store their honey in a honeycomb.

One bee will make one teaspoon of honey in its lifetime.

45

Beautiful butterflies

Butterflies flutter around gardens and meadows, feeding on the nectar from flowers. Their wings are made up of tiny colored scales, giving them their trademark patterns.

Butterflies can use their feet to taste the flowers they land on!

The Buddleia plant is known as "butterfly bush" because butterflies love to drink nectar from its flowers.

COLOR in the butterflies. Then add sticker butterflies to fill the pages.

Facts about...

Butterfly lifecycle

The beautiful butterflies we see in the yard start life looking very different. They go through three stages—egg, caterpillar, and pupa—before finally emerging as butterflies in a process called **metamorphosis.**

1 **Butterflies** lay their **eggs** on plants. The caterpillars start eating as soon as they hatch.

Caterpillars **2** eat nonstop and grow quickly. They shed their skin several times as they grow.

3 **The caterpillar** then transforms into a **pupa**. It attaches itself to a plant and forms a case around itself.

Finally, **4** a beautiful butterfly emerges from the case.

47

In the air

FIND and stick down the right stickers for the winged creatures below.

Birds and insects aren't the only animals that can take to the air. Some fish and squirrels can glide through the air, too.

Parrot

Parrot

Dragonfly

Bald eagle

Schreiber's bat

Butterfly

Barn owl

Cardinal beetle

48

COLOR these beautiful birds, plus a beetle, flying fish, and gliding squirrel.

Hummingbird

Toucan

Flying squirrel

Scarab beetle

Lorikeets

Mallard duck

Kingfisher

Flying fish

49

Into the wild

Take an adventure into the wild. In this chapter you will meet monkeys, bears, crocodiles, big cats, jungle animals, and creatures of the deep. Watch out for the scary ones!

FIND these pictures on pages 51–64 and write the page numbers in the boxes.

page _____

page _____

page _____

page _____

page _____

page _____

page _____

Don't forget to put your stickers in first.

what do I eat?

Buffalo
Buffaloes are **grazers**. They live in savanna grassland and move in herds looking for food.

My food is in bowl...

Monkey
Monkeys have a diet of nuts, seeds, and **fruit**. When it's available, they love this yellow food...

My food is in bowl...

FIND each animal's food by following the paths to the bowls.

A

B

C

D

Otter
Otters spend most of their time in **water**, so it makes sense that fish is on their menu.

My food is in bowl...

Elephant
Elephants are **big** mammals, so they need to eat a lot each day to fill them up.

My food is in bowls...

Panda
Pandas eat bamboo, but because many bamboo forests have been cut down, pandas have become **endangered**.

My food is in bowl...

51

Pygmy marmoset

Ape & monkey gallery

Monkeys and apes are both good climbers and mainly live in trees. The way to tell them apart is that monkeys have tails and apes don't.

MATCH stickers to the frames to create a gallery and add monkey visitors beneath.

Howler monkeys can use their tails as an extra limb to grasp things.

Capuchins are intelligent monkeys that use rocks as tools to open nuts.

Black and white colobus are good at scampering along branches.

Macaques have long cheek pouches that hold as much food as their stomachs do.

Orangutans are apes with long arms that they use to swing in trees.

Red colobus only eat plant foods such as leaves and flowers.

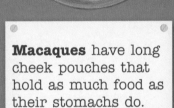

Orangutan

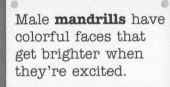

Male **mandrills** have colorful faces that get brighter when they're excited.

Chimpanzees are very smart apes. They can use sticks and rocks as tools.

American black bear

This bear lives in North American forests. It eats mostly roots, shoots, buds, and fruits.

Giant panda

A fussy eater, it will only eat few types of bamboo and meat. It is black and white and lives in China.

Sun bear

The Sun bear of Southeast Asia has an amazingly long tongue to lick honey and insects out of holes in trees.

Spectacled bear

This bear is so named because it has rings of pale fur around its eyes. It is South America's only bear.

Sloth bear This bear lives in the forests of India and feeds at night on termites, which it sucks up noisily through its lips.

Where's the bear?

North America

South America

MATCH the bear stickers to the shapes. Then find out where they live by looking at the map.

Brown bear

The brown bear lives in North America, Asia, and Europe. It comes into contact with humans regularly and is incredibly dangerous.

Asiatic black bear

Found in the Himalaya Mountains and other parts of Asia, this bear is a good climber. It is known as "Moon bear" because of the crescent-shaped patch on its chest.

54

With their large, powerful bodies and thick, shaggy fur, bears are built for survival in the world's toughest places—from jungle-covered mountaintops to the frozen Arctic.

Europe

Asia

Africa

Australia

No bears live in the continent of Africa.

Although it's called a bear, the koala isn't a bear at all.

Polar bear
The biggest and deadliest type of bear, the polar bear eats mainly meat. It lives around the North Pole.

Koala bear
Australia's koala isn't a bear at all—it's really a marsupial (a mammal that carries babies in a pouch).

55

COLOR
in the fish and draw your own sea creature in the space.

Dolphins communicate with each other by clicking.

Lion's mane jellyfish can extend to a size that's longer than a whale.

flesh-eating fish.

Great white sharks are the largest

Sunfish are the heaviest bony fish.

Conger eel are long, snakelike fish.

Sailfish can move as fast as 60 mph (100 kph).

Tuna can live to 35 years old.

TRUE OR FALSE?
A BLUE WHALE'S TONGUE WEIGHS AS MUCH AS AN ELEPHANT.

ocean creatures

The four oceans cover more than two-thirds of the Earth's surface and are where some of the largest and strangest animals on the planet live.

Giant squid are hunted by sperm whales.

Giant Squid

Draw your own ocean creature

Manta rays fly through the water.

Their fins flap like birds' wings.

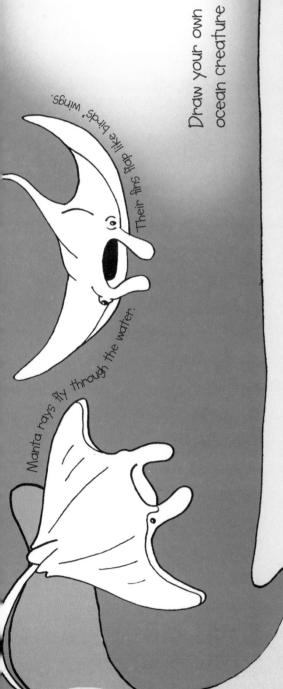

Spider crabs reach 12ft (4 m) wide.

Sperm whales can hold their breath for up to 90 minutes.

Facts about...

The deep

The deepest parts of the ocean are pitch black and the fish that live there make their own light. They use it to lure smaller fish to their death.

Cat attack!

They might look like bigger versions of cute house cats, but their combination of size, speed, and strength makes big cats some of the most dangerous animals on Earth.

FINISH these big cats using stickers. Then name the big cats based on the clues.

1

Write the name of each big cat in the right box.

Can you come up with your own big cat fur pattern?

Facts about...

Roaring

Of the big cats, only lions, jaguars, tigers, and leopards are able to **roar**. The species known as small cats—such as cheetahs and cougars—can't roar at all.

I live on the plains of Africa. I'm sometimes called King of the Jungle, and my thick mane is used to scare away enemies.

2 Lion _ _ _ _ _ _ _

USE THESE CLUES TO NAME THE BIG CATS.

Lion

Panther

Jaguar

I'm the largest of the big cats, and I can be found in parts of Asia. My dark stripes keep me hidden when I'm hunting in the tall, thick grass.

3 Tiger _ _ _ _ _

I'm not actually a separate species of big cat; I'm a black version of a leopard or jaguar. You can find me in Asia, Africa, and the Americas.

4 Panther _ _ _ _ _ _ _ _

Tiger

Killer crocs

Crocodiles and alligators are cold-blooded killers that lurk hidden in rivers and swamps. One bite from their powerful jaws and there's no escape!

To help them see in the dark, their vertical pupils can open wide

SEE how much you know about crocodiles and alligators in the quiz below.

True or false?

1
Alligators can live for more than 100 years.

TRUE   FALSE

2
Saltwater crocodiles have the strongest bite of all crocodiles and alligators.

TRUE   FALSE

3
Crocodiles and alligators can survive up to a year without eating.

TRUE   FALSE

How to tell a crocodile from an alligator

Alligator

- Shorter, wider, U-shaped snout
- Dark in color
- Only live in freshwater environments
- Bottom teeth disappear when mouth closes

Crocodile

- Long, narrow, V-shaped snout
- Pale in color
- Live in both saltwater and freshwater environments
- Bottom teeth stay visible when mouth closes

Facts about...

Killer jaws

The muscles that close a crocodile's mouth are strong but the muscles that open it are weak. This means it's easy to hold it's mouth closed, but very hard to escape if it bites!

The strongest part of a crocodile's body is its long, muscular tail.

Quizzes

4

Ancestors of crocodiles lived at the same time as the dinosaurs.

TRUE   FALSE

5

Crocodiles and alligators never stop growing.

TRUE   FALSE

6

Their eggs hatch into males if they're kept warm and females if they're cold.

TRUE   FALSE

61

Deep in the jungle

Only about 6 percent of the land on Earth is covered in tropical forest. But the jungle is so full of life that more than half of all known species can be found living there.

Emergent layer

High above the canopy, tropical birds such as macaws can be found in large numbers.

STICK

these jungle animals from all over the world into the right layers.

Canopy

Gibbons, monkeys, sloths, and bush babies love the canopy. This layer is full of life.

Understory

The understory, which is covered with palms and vines, is full of butterflies and tree frogs.

Forest floor

The humid forest floor is home to species such as jaguars, capybara, tapirs, and insects.

Forest layers

Forests are divided into **four main layers**, each one containing different animals and plants. Most animals generally stay in their own layer.

Facts about ...

63

Coral reef

Stick these creepy-crawlies on **page 3.**

These bugs go on **pages 4–5.**

Stag beetle   June bug   Ladybug   Desert locust   Grasshopper   Katydid

Hawk moth caterpillar   Swallowtail caterpillar   Fritillary caterpillar

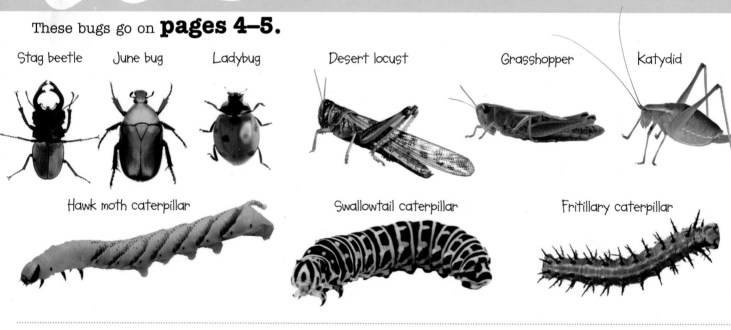

Stick these flies and spiders on **pages 8–9.**

Stick these snakes on
pages 10–11.

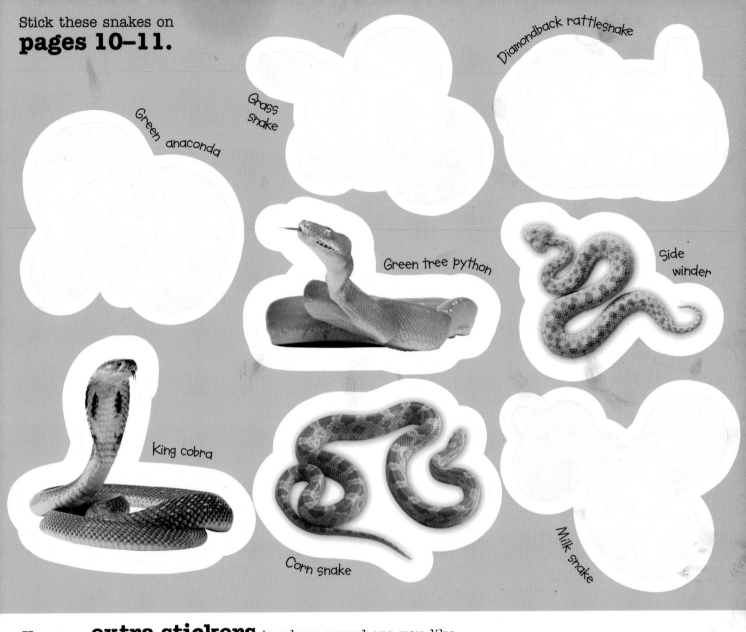

Diamondback rattlesnake

Grass snake

Green anaconda

Green tree python

Side winder

King cobra

Corn snake

Milk snake

Here are **extra stickers** to place anywhere you like.

Use these colorful geckos to decorate **page 12.**

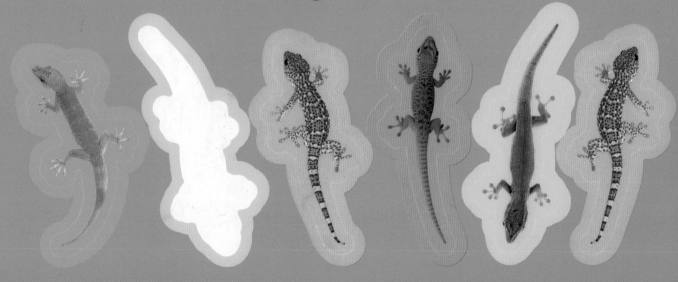

Use these stickers to complete the puzzle on **page 13.**

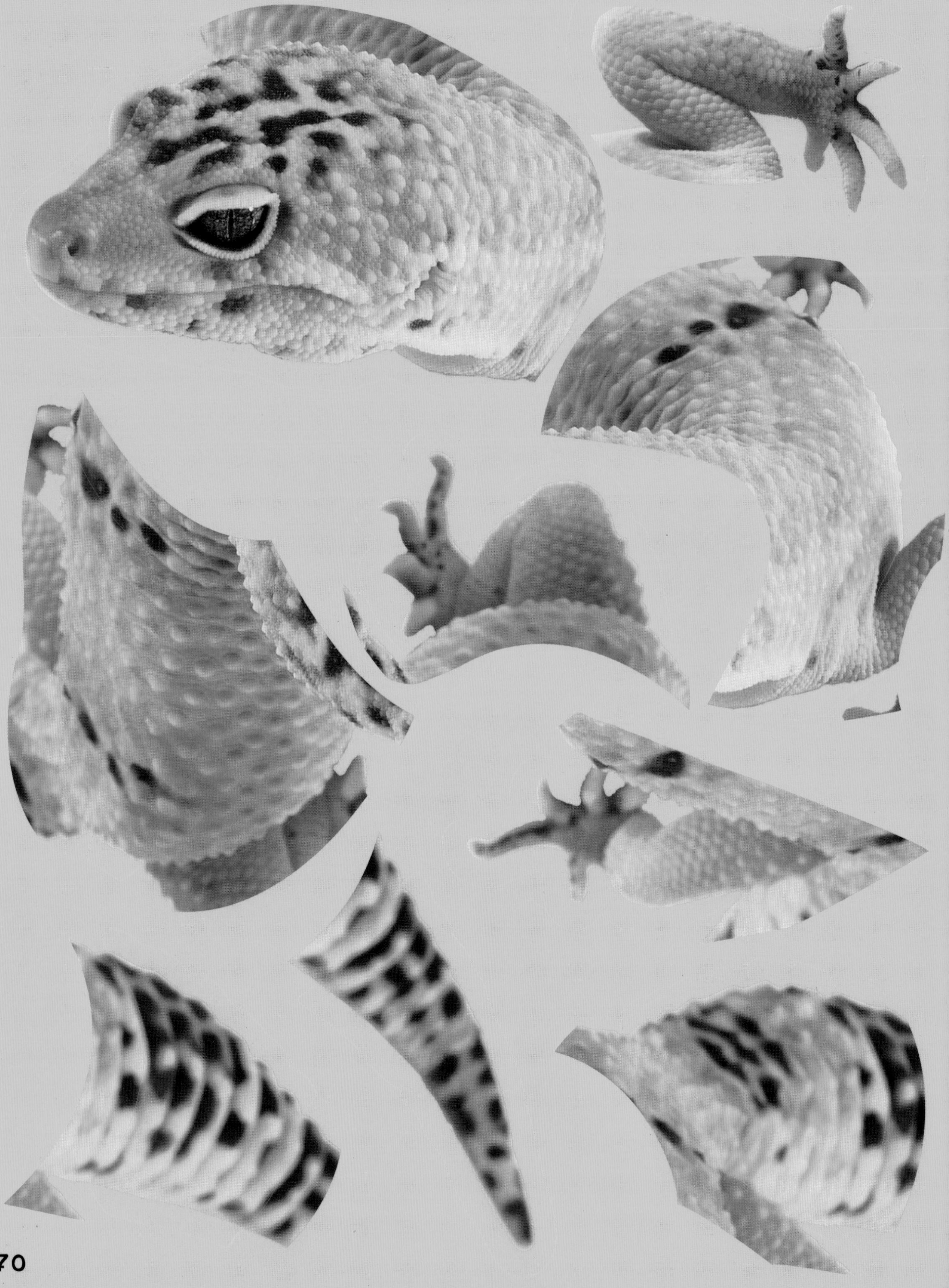